This book belongs to:

_____

_____

To Len, the marvellous engineer, and all young engineers to come M.B.

To Finn, Scarlett and Madeleine B.C.

First American Edition 2021
Kane Miller, A Division of EDC Publishing

First published 2021 by Walker Books Ltd
87 Vauxhall Walk, London SE11 5HJ
Text © 2021 Moira Butterfield
Illustrations © 2021 Bryony Clarkson

For information contact:
Kane Miller, A Division of EDC Publishing
5402 S. 122nd E. Ave, Tulsa, OK 74146
www.kanemiller.com
www.myubam.com

Library of Congress Control Number: 2021930467

Printed in China

1 2 3 4 5 6 7 8 9 10
ISBN: 978-1-68464-244-1

WHEELS!
ALL ABOUT TRANSPORT

Moira
Butterfield

illustrated by
Bryony
Clarkson

Kane Miller
A DIVISION OF EDC PUBLISHING

Contents

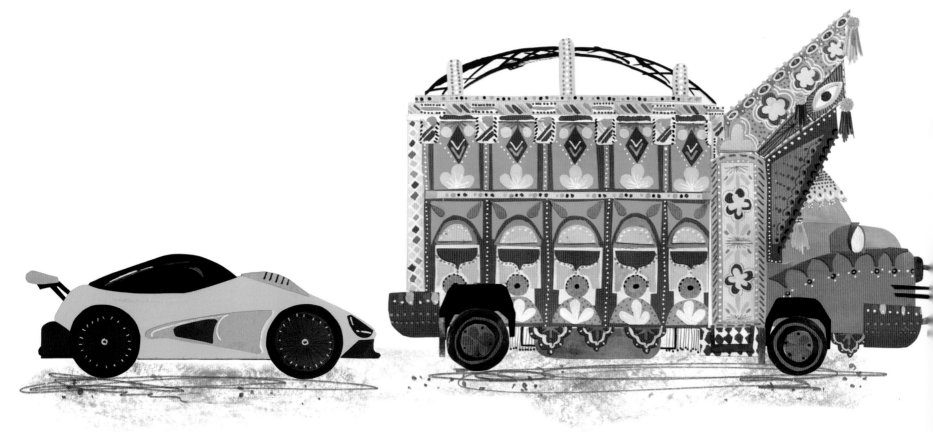

Shiny, purring, whirring cars.

Rusty, dusty, dented cars.

Speckled with the rain cars.

Creeping down the lane cars.

Doggies in the back cars.

Crazy flying bat cars...

The next few pages are all about cars!

Road Trip

2 Through a tunnel.

1 Turn the car onto the road.

5 Over some bumps.

8

3 On with the wipers.

4 Across a bridge.

6 Where are we going? Home!

SUPERHERO SUPERCAR

4ROAR

Here comes a powerful supercar.

It's low to the ground, like a crouching lion.

It starts by purrrrrring slowly along.

Then...

RROAR!

MECHANIC MEL

Is your car **coughing?** Is your car **clanking?**

Leave it to Mechanic Mel.

She'll take a look and stroke her chin,

then open up her toolbox, to find:

bolts,

spark plugs,

wheel nuts,

grips,

socket wrench,

ratchets,

hammers,

& oil cans...

When Mechanic Mel has fixed your car

she'll open up another box:

her lunch!

(There are about 30,000 separate parts in an ordinary car. No wonder Mechanic Mel needs lots of tools.)

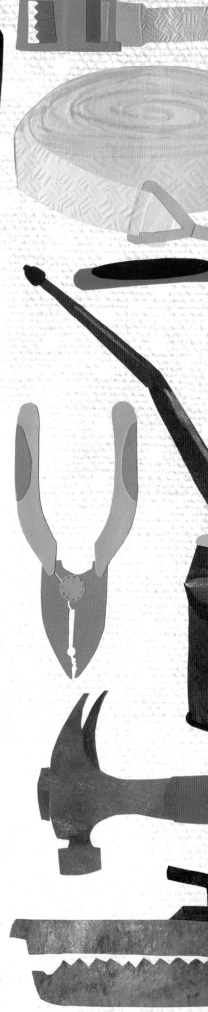

CO·1XA

GAS

32

4

8AFP-3

5

The Car Parade

Every year, big crowds gather in Houston, Texas, for the Art Car Parade.

This parade has a car covered with grass,

and a car that's like a bunch of flowers ...

a dinosaur car,

an octopus car,

and even a sheep car!

Baaa!

SPEEDY SUPERSTARS

Zooooooom!

The world's fastest race cars take part in Formula One races.

Zooooooom!

A cheetah is the fastest animal runner, but a Formula One car can go three times as fast.

PIT STOP

Zooooooom!

Mechanics can replace the wheels in about two seconds — roughly as long as it takes to blink your eyes five times.

START

FINISH

It only takes a few seconds for a super-speedy Formula One car to brake and **stop**.

Future Cars

What will cars look like in the future?

Some cars won't need a driver. They'll be controlled by computers and cameras.

And you'll be able to call for a driverless minicar, to take you on short trips. It will zip along when you call and say:

"Hello! I'm your minicar for today."

Car wheels might be spherical, like soccer balls –

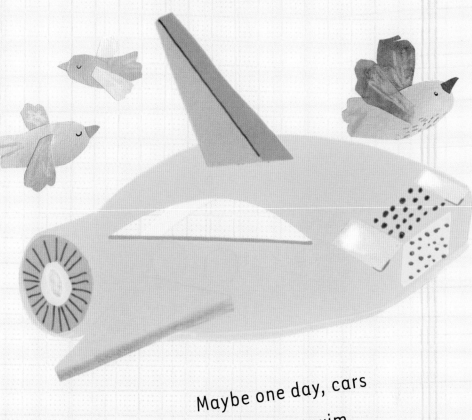

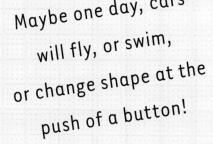

to swivel in different directions.

Maybe one day, cars
will fly, or swim,
or change shape at the
push of a button!

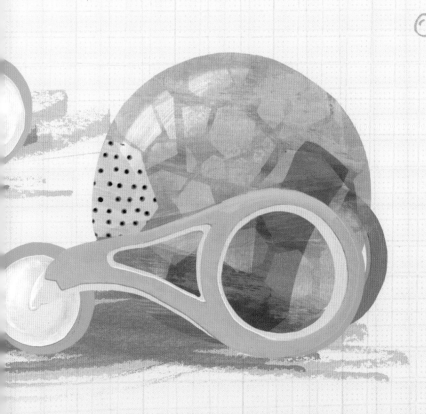

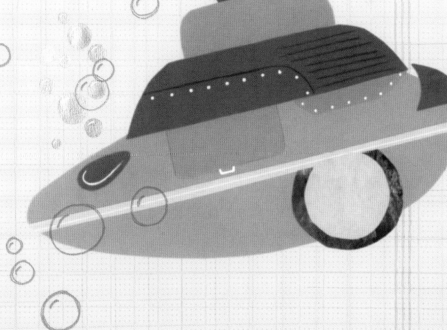

Plug in for

the Planet

Soon we will all be taking rides in electric cars, buses, and trucks — to make the world a cleaner place. They run on batteries, not on gasoline, and they don't make fumes as they drive along.

Let's plug in for the planet!

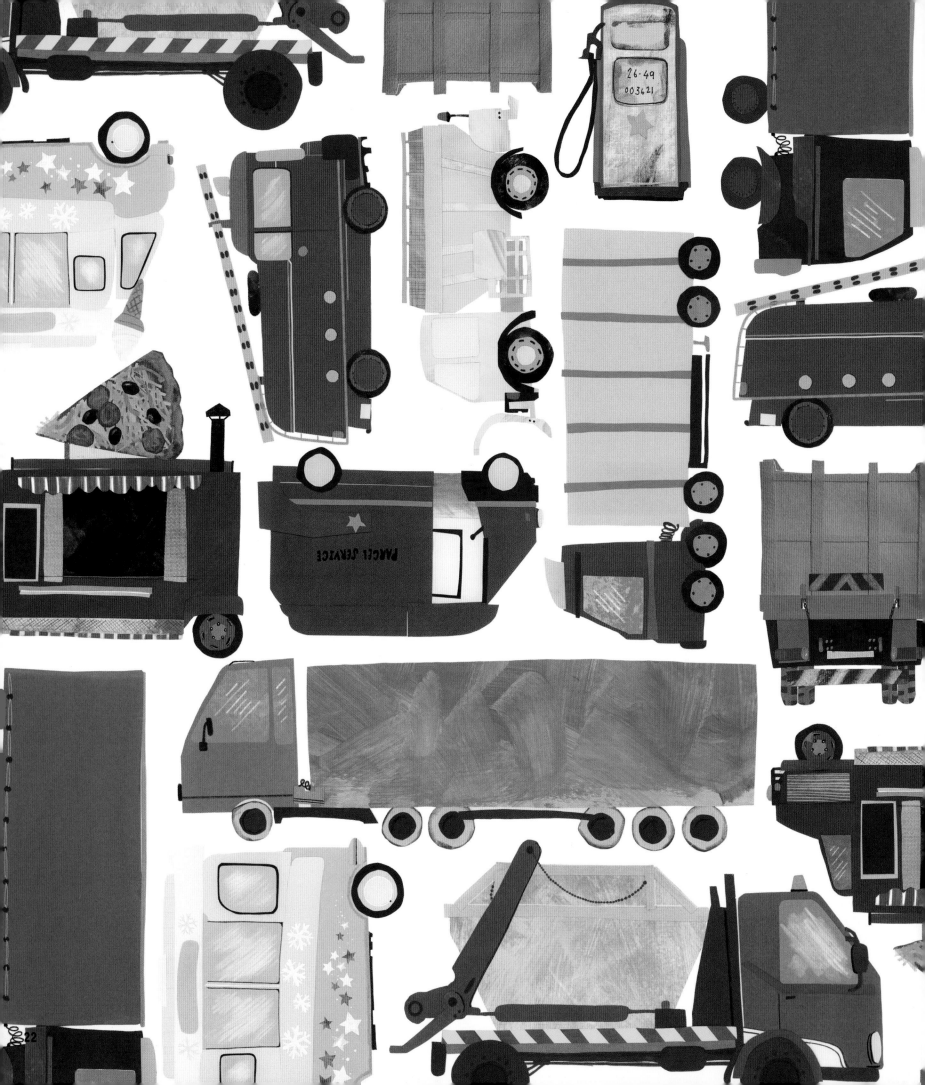

Big fat wheels, a-rollin', rollin',

Load in the back, a-haulin', haulin',

Engine rumblin', rumblin', rumblin',

Eating up the long, long road…

These pages are all about

trucks!

SMELLY TRUCK

Along comes the smelly truck,

here to take your garbage.

Runny stuff and slimy stuff

and yucky stuff you didn't eat,

getting smellier in the heat.

Cheesy, moldy, slippery, squishy...

Yuck...

Hey! Don't make fun of the smelly truck for eating up YOUR stinky muck.

Give the truck a break day. Don't throw so much away!

Truck **Race**

Trucks take part in the world's longest motor race — the Dakar Rally.
It lasts for fourteen days across South America.

And they're off!

The trucks must drive through
swampy mud ... *sploosh!*

Along rocky mountain tracks ...

bump, bump, bumpety, bump!

Over giant sand dunes ...

hold on tight!

All to make it to the finish line with the fastest time. *Hooray!*

Moving Day

"Anything else to pack?"

"Not much. Only the …

TV, the tools,

the pots, the pans,

the plant on the sill,

the cat's basket,

the dog's bowl,

and the drum kit."

"That's it. A perfect fit."

"Let's go to the new house! Byeee!"

"Wait a minute."

Squeeeeeal!

Vehicle reversing.

Vehicle reversing.

"We forgot something.

The new address!"

THIS
WAY UP

Record Trucks

Road trains are the world's longest trucks — the longest ever had more than 900 wheels.

Mining trucks have the world's biggest wheels: each one weighs as much as an African elephant.

The **Shockwave jet truck** is one of the world's speediest trucks. It has THREE airplane jet engines!

TOP-TEN TRUCKS

Airport truck. Gritter truck. Logging truck. Milk truck. Builders' truck. Circus truck. Delivery truck. Pickup truck. Fuel truck. Stunt truck.

Ready, set,
JUMP TRUCK!

Pack That Truck

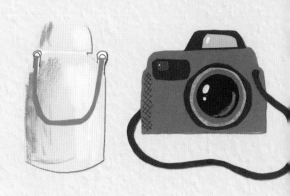

What will you pack before you go

on a mountain rescue, out in the snow?

What will you pack

on a rooftop rack

for a trek along

a jungle track?

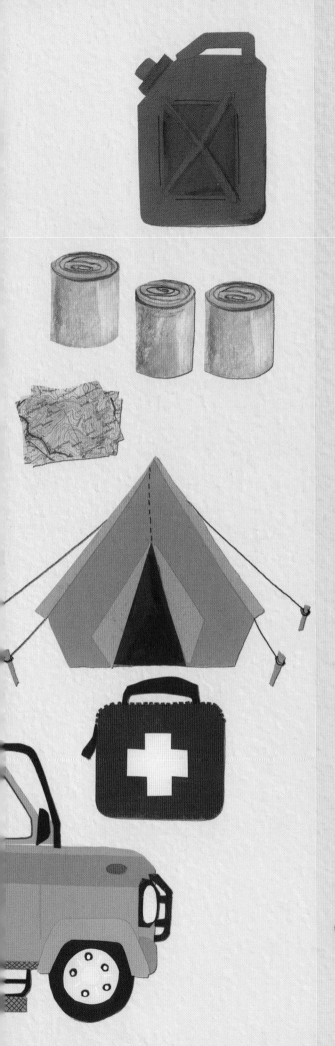

What will you pack for a drive in space,

across the Moon, and back to base?

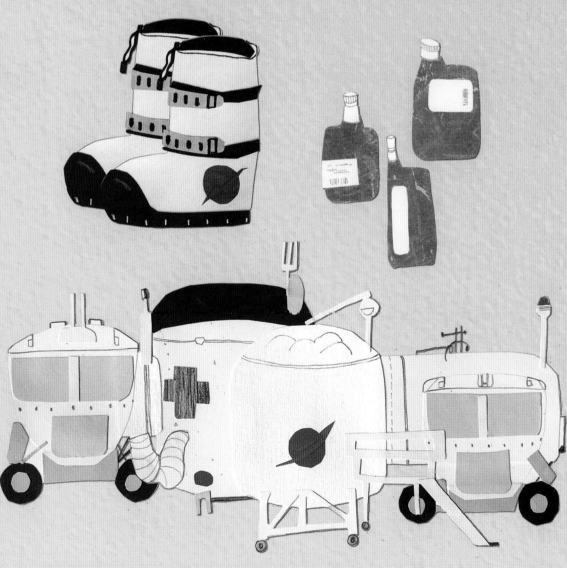

35

TOW TRUCK

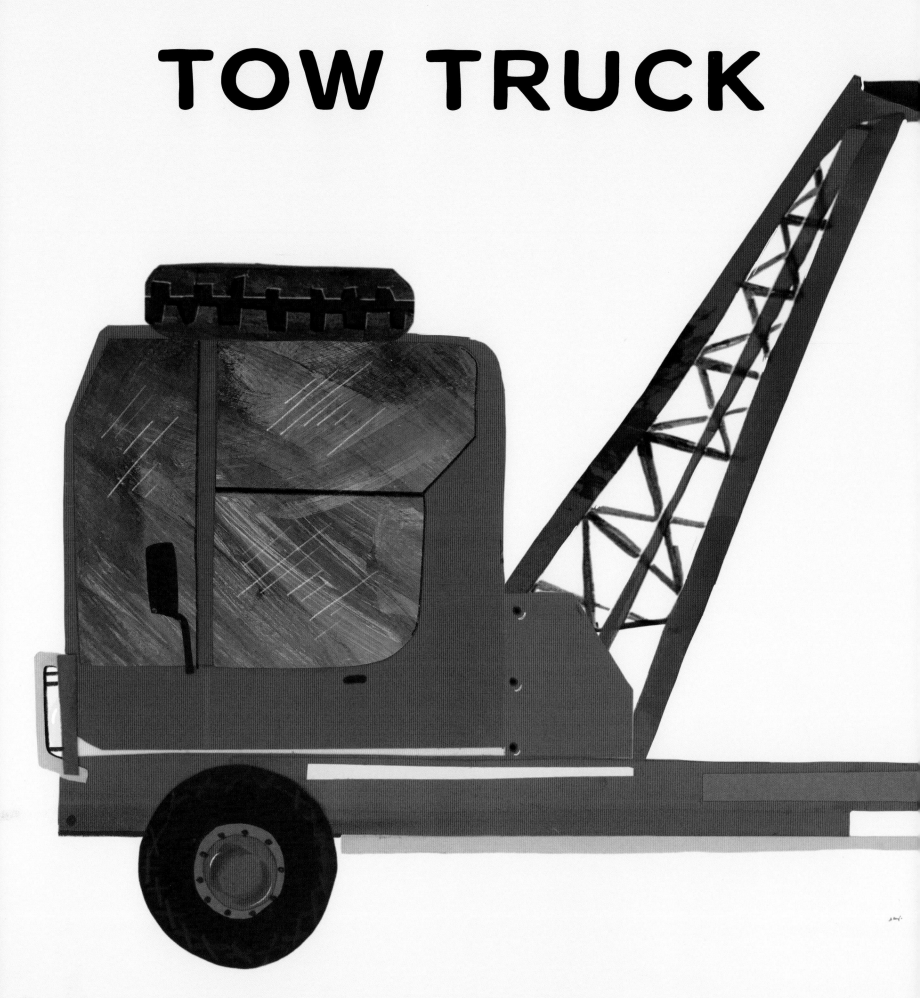

The platform lowers ...
hiss, clonk.

Then up it tips —
whoosh, bop —
to make a handy ramp.

A chain unwinds —
clank, clank —
and fixes to the broken car.

The chain winds back —
rumble, click —
and pulls the car on board.

It's time to go.
Vroom! Vroom!

Let's get that car back home.

Trucks of the World!

Trucks look different around the world...

In Pakistan, trucks are sometimes decorated with carvings, paintings, and bells. They have a nickname — jingle trucks — because they jingle as they move.

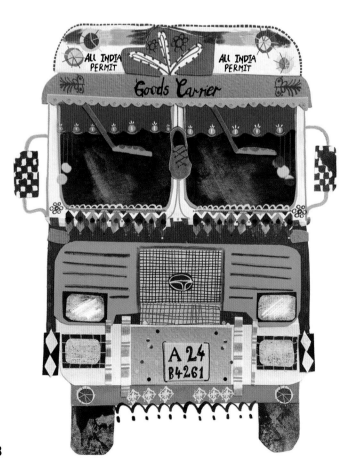

In India, trucks are often painted with lucky symbols. They might also have a shoe hung somewhere, to keep bad luck away.

In Japan, trucks called dekotora have lots of shiny metal and blazing lights. At night, they look like spaceships driving along!

In Peru, truckers like to paint pictures of animals, such as lions and bears, on the backs of their trucks.

Mixing concrete. Digging holes.

Plowing. Planting. Loading hay.

Racing to the hospital.

Driving children off to school…

These pages are about ALL KINDS of wheels!

TALK TRACTOR

A tractor has a superpowerful engine, but it's not for going fast. It's for pulling heavy farm equipment.

plow

A **plow** turns over the earth.

A **planter** sows seeds in rows.

A **baler** picks up a grassy crop and squeezes it into handy bales.

A **trailer** carries all sorts of things.

Plow, planter, baler, trailer.

Now you can talk tractor!

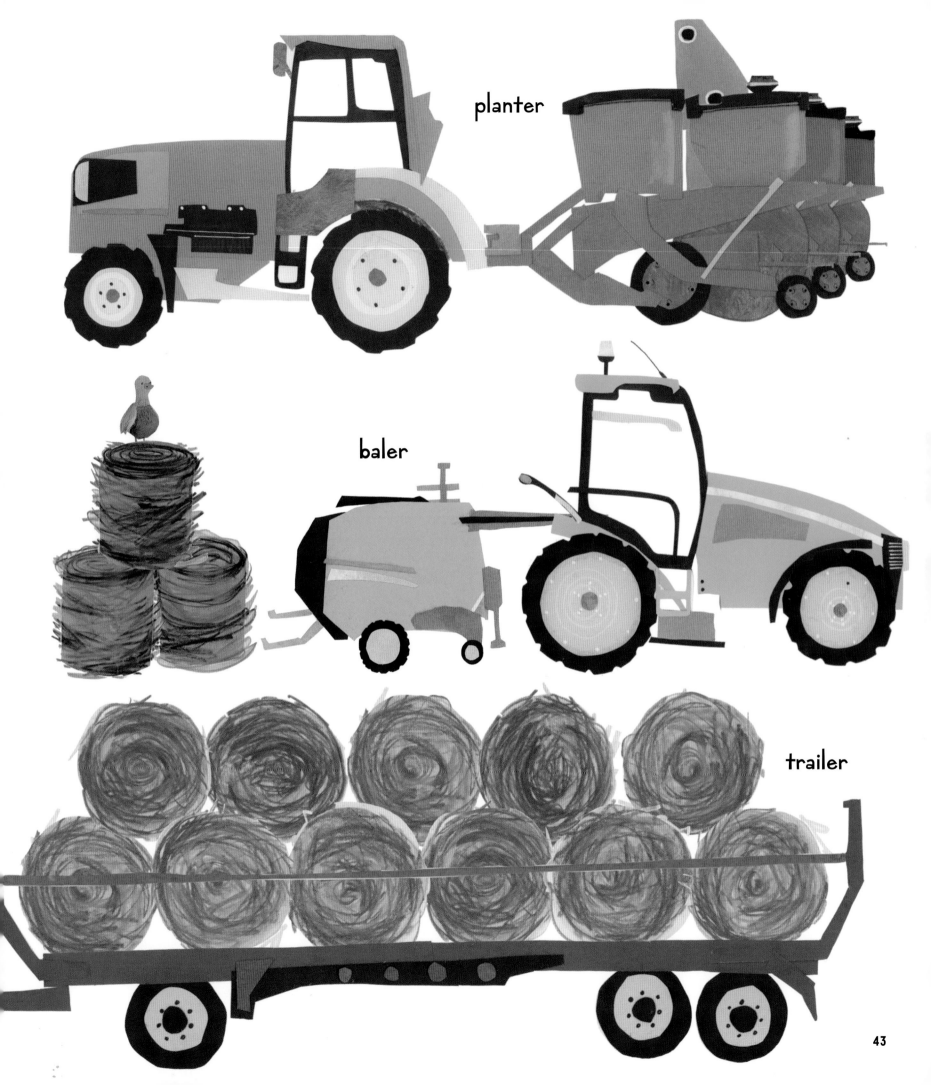

planter

baler

trailer

Your Turn

Today it's YOUR turn on the tractor.

Drive around
the duck pond,
where ducks are
bobbing.
QUACK, QUACK.
Give them a wave.

Drive through
the farmyard,
past the chickens.
CLUCK, CLUCK.
Give them a wave.

Turn through
the gateway,
where the cows
are grazing.
MOO, MOO.
Give them a wave.

Pull all the levers. Push all the buttons.
Today's the day that YOU'RE in charge.

45

AROUND THE WORLD

IN FIRE TRUCKS

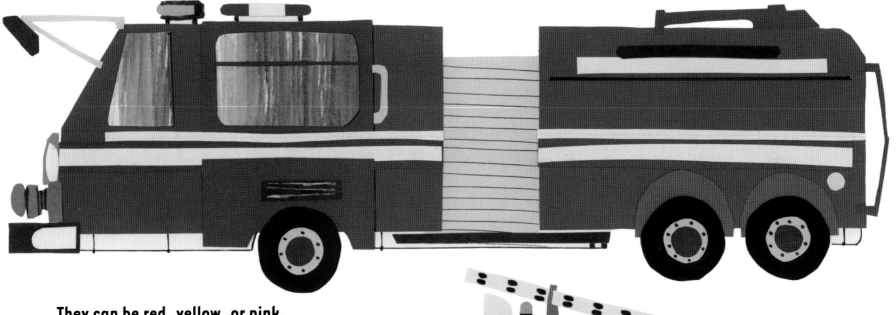

They can be red, yellow, or pink,

blue, green, orange, or white.

They make different noises, too, like:

whoooooooo whoooooooOO,

or: nee naw nee naw.

But they are ALL shiny, with flashing lights.

And they ALL carry ladders and pumps and tools —

and brave firefighters ready for action.

Put on your gear:

fireproof clothing, helmet, boots, and gloves...
OK.

Check the fire truck:

hoses working, ladder, siren, lights...
OK.

Time to practice:

climb a ladder, spray the water around...
OK.

Call the Captain.

"Can you hear me? We are on our way."
OK.

You've done your training for the day.

Here's your firefighter badge.
OK!

Fire Truck Training

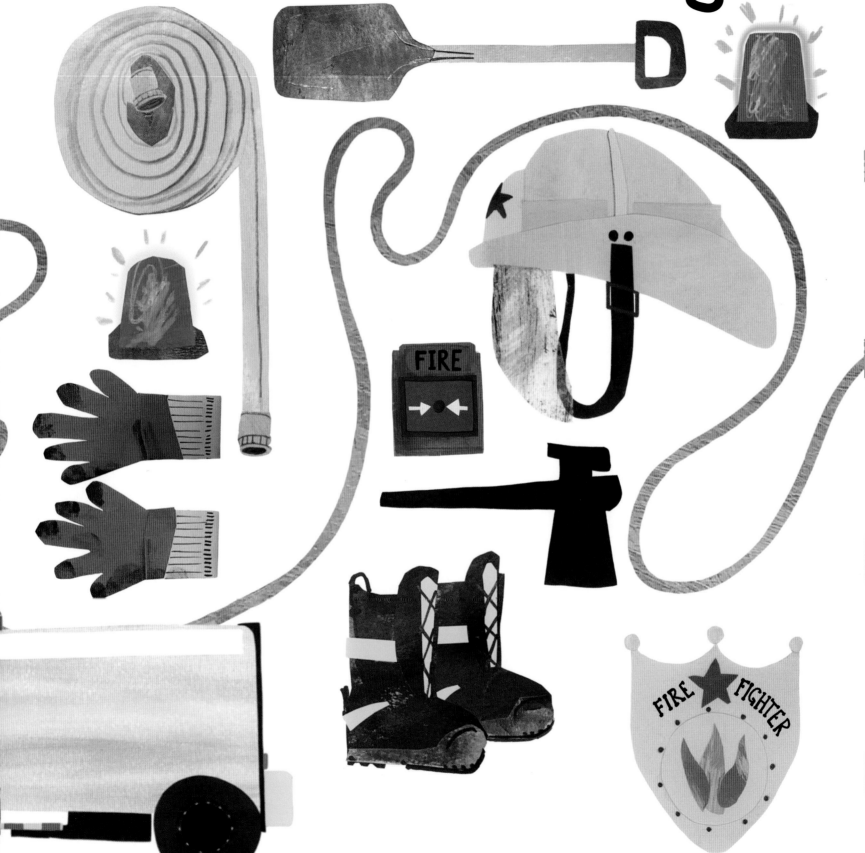

HERE TO HELP

When people need help, police cars and ambulances **zooooooom** to where the trouble is — but which one would:

... help someone with a broken arm?

... investigate a loud alarm?

... take someone to see a nurse?

... chase a thief who stole a purse?

... get to the hospital on the double?

... sort out some traffic trouble?

DIG, *Push*, **TIP**, *Stir*

DIG, DIG, DIG a hole
with the excavator.
Its metal arm scoops up the earth
to dig, dig a hole.

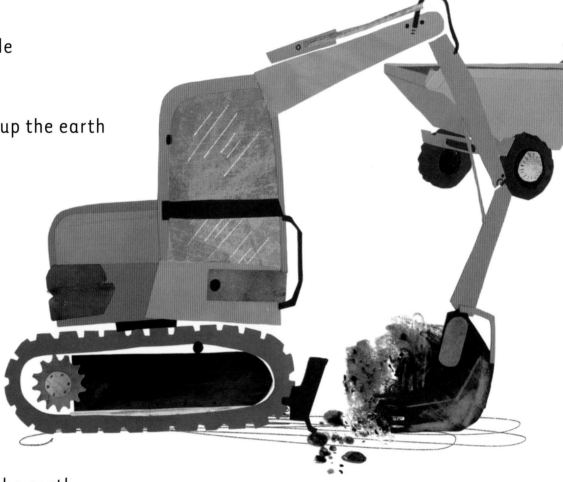

Push, Push, Push the earth
with the strong bulldozer.
Its blade is like a giant's hand
to push, push the earth.

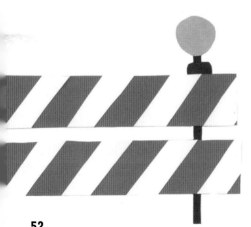

TIP, **TIP**, **TIP** the stones
with the nifty dump truck.
It raises up to pour a load
and tip, tip the stones.

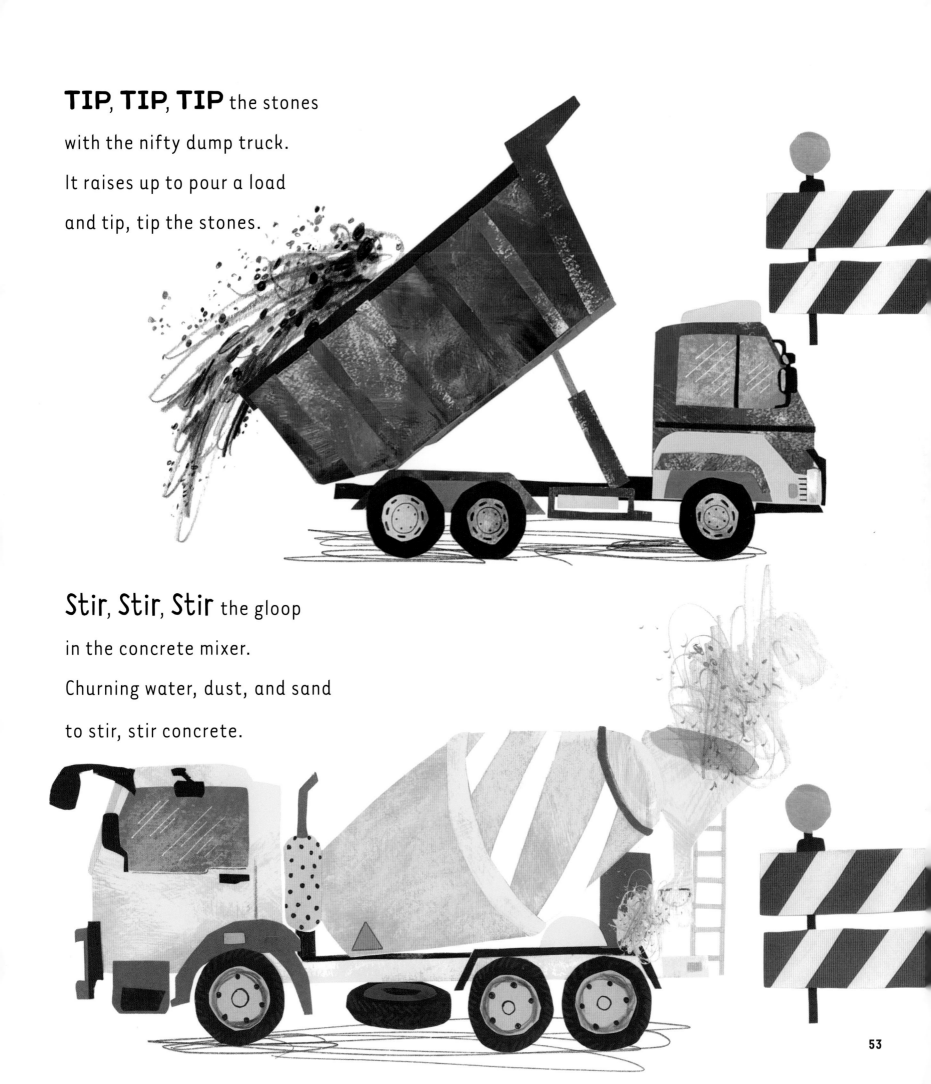

Stir, Stir, Stir the gloop
in the concrete mixer.
Churning water, dust, and sand
to stir, stir concrete.

Crane

The **crane cab's** connected to a ... **crane truck.**

The **crane truck's** connected to a ... **crane arm.**

The **crane arm's** connected to a ... **long chain.**

The **long chain's** connected to a ... **big hook.**

The **big hook's** connected to a ...

wrecking ball.

Wham!

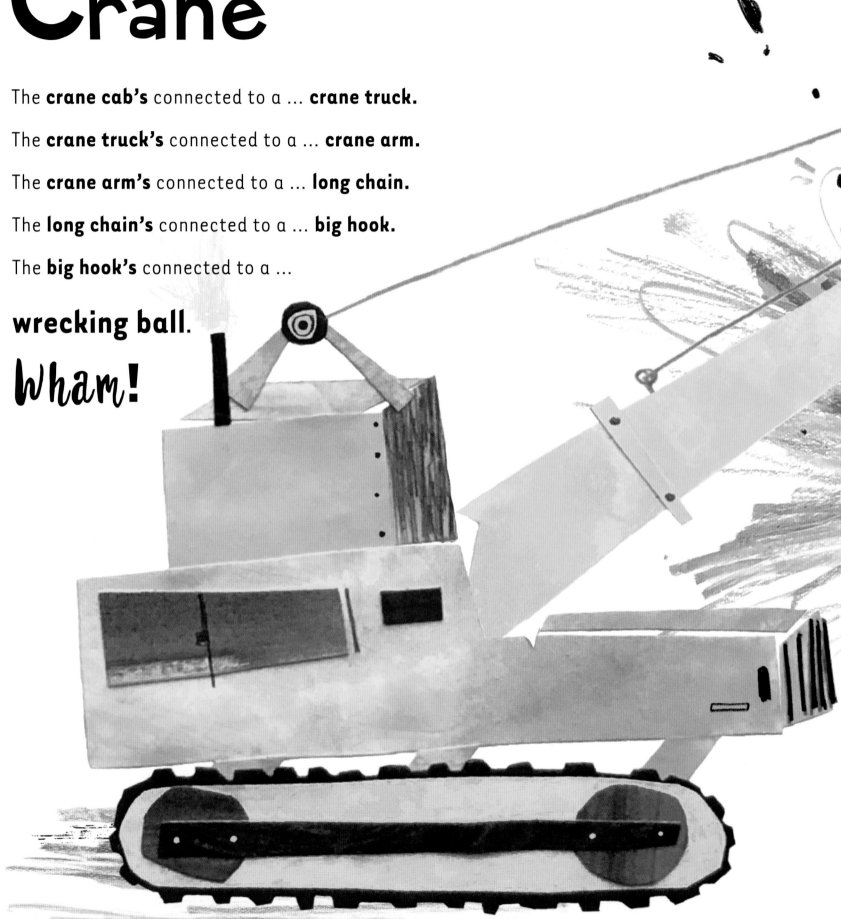

How to Fix a Road

Sometimes a road gets **lumpy** and **bumpy** and it needs a nice new surface.

The old road surface is scraped off by one machine, which empties

the rubble into a dump truck to take it away.

Another machine covers the road in new asphalt — a mixture of sand, stones, and sticky black tar.

A heavy road roller squashes the asphalt down, so there are no more lumps and bumps.

When the asphalt has cooled, it's ready for cars to drive on again!

Ride the Bus

Chiva buses like this one give rides in Ecuador, South America. They earned their name by climbing steep mountain roads, just like a "chiva" — a goat!

Bananas, peppers,

berries, melons.

Yellow, orange, green, and red.

Colors glowing in the sunshine,

on the way to market.

Climb aboard the

rainbow chiva.

Chat in Spanish. Hi. Hola.

¡Vámonos! Let's get going...

On the way to market.

Old Bus

First the bus took kids to school, as they made funny faces.
Then it ferried tourists around to visit lovely places.

Next it carried soccer players, off to play a game.

And then it was an airport bus, driving to a plane.

And when its engine got worn out and could no longer run,
it became a bus for chickens, sitting in the sun.

Cluck!

Traffic Jam

Old car. New car. Little car. Big car. Race car. Royal car. Slow tractor. Fast taxi.

Trailer full of muck. Pizza truck…

Duck?

Brakes on… SLAM! Traffic jam!

Around the next bend it's ...

The
End